449
Stupid Things
Democrats
Have Said

449
Stupid Things
Democrats
Have Said

Ted Rueter

**Andrews McMeel
Publishing**

Kansas City

449 Stupid Things Democrats Have Said copyright
© 2004 by Ted Rueter. All rights reserved. Printed in
the United States of America. No part of this book may
be used or reproduced in any manner whatsoever
without written permission except in the case of
reprints in the context of reviews. For information, write
Andrews McMeel Publishing, an Andrews McMeel
Universal company, 4520 Main Street, Kansas City,
Missouri 64111.

ISBN: 0-7407-4370-8

Library of Congress Control Number: 2003114760

04 05 06 07 08 VAI 10 9 8 7 6 5 4 3 2 1

ATTENTION: SCHOOLS AND BUSINESSES

Andrews McMeel books are available at quantity
discounts with bulk purchase for educational,
business, or sales promotional use. For information,
please write to: Special Sales Department, Andrews
McMeel Publishing, 4520 Main Street, Kansas City,
Missouri 64111.

Action

"I'm a man of action. And unlike Schwarzenegger, I never had a stunt man do my hard work."

> —Al Sharpton (2004 presidential candidate), during the Congressional Black Caucus presidential debate

Adversaries

"Better to have 'em inside the tent pissin' out than outside pissin' in."

> —Lyndon Johnson (president, 1963–1969), on why he kept J. Edgar Hoover as head of the FBI

Affirmative Action

"We've been told we had three minutes. My good friend Senator Edwards spoke for five. So Joe Lieberman told me that, in the spirit of affirmative action, I get seven."

> —Al Sharpton, at a presidential candidates' forum

⭐ African Americans

"African Americans watch the same news at night that ordinary Americans do."

> —Bill Clinton (president, 1993–2001), on Black Entertainment Television

"If the percentage of minorities that's in your state has anything to do with how you connect with African-American voters, then Trent Lott would be Martin Luther King."

> —Howard Dean (2004 presidental candidate), asked if the fact that only 0.5 percent of Vermont residents are black didn't make it difficult for him to understand the black community

⭐ African Diplomats

"Everybody likes to go to Geneva. I used to do it for the Law of the Sea conferences and you'd find these potentates from down in Africa, you know, rather than eating each other, they'd just come up and get a good square meal in Geneva."

> —Ernest Hollings (senator from South Carolina, 1965–2004)

🐴 America

"Of course, I love many things American, including the food. You know, I used to work in a Howard Johnson's restaurant."

—Hillary Rodham Clinton (first lady, 1993–2001)

"God bless the America we are trying to create."

—Hillary Rodham Clinton

🐴 Answers

"I should have had a circuitous answer that was a nonanswer."

—Geraldine Ferraro (1984 vice-presidential nominee), on her intended replies to media inquiries about her family's finances

🐴 Antenna

"I have a pretty good antenna for people who are chauvinistic or sexist or patronizing toward women."

—Hillary Rodham Clinton

🫏 Anticipation

"I remember you telling me earlier today that you were looking forward to not talking much today. I was looking forward to it, too."

> —Randy Ewing (Louisiana state senator, 1988–2000), to Louisiana state senator John Hainkel

🫏 Arm Wrestling

"If there's enough money, I'll try it. Sure."

> —Terry McAuliffe (chairman, Democratic National Committee), on the idea of arm wrestling Arnold Schwarzenegger for charity

🫏 Arnold

"Don't run. You will be terminated."

> —Willie Brown (mayor of San Francisco, 1996–2004), on Arnold Schwarzenegger's prospects as a gubernatorial candidate

"Ever see the movie *Twins*? I guess I'm Danny Devito."

> —Cruz Bustamante (2003 California gubernatorial candidate), referring to a movie starring Arnold Schwarzennegger

"Schwarzenegger is going to find out that unlike a Hollywood movie set, the bullets coming at him in this campaign are going to be real bullets."

> —Bob Mulholland (political director, California Democratic Party), during the 2003 gubernatorial recall campaign. Mulholland apologized for this remark.

"He's a sissy is what I'm saying. He's a scaredy cat."

> —Richie Ross (strategist for Cruz Bustamante), on Arnold Schwarzenegger's failure to participate in debates

"He's a brilliant actor, but what makes Republicans think he could do well in politics? Of course, it's hard to argue with Arnold when you're hanging upside down by the ankles."

> —Ted Kennedy (senator from Massachusetts, 1963–)

★ Artillery

"I've got recon out there. I've got some heavy
artillery that can come in. I've got good logistics,
and I've got strategic mobility."

> —Wesley Clark (2004 presidential
> candidate), a retired four-star general,
> asked if his late entry into the presidential
> race didn't present problems

★ John Ashcroft

"He is a living, breathing troglodyte who happens to
run the Justice Department."

> —Chris Lehane (John Kerry's presidential
> campaign adviser)

★ Aspirations

"I think I would like to be a better dancer."

> —Al Gore (vice president, 1993–2001)

★ Audiences

"The best audience is intelligent, well educated, and
a little drunk."

> —Alben Barkley (vice president, 1949–1953)

 Back–Scratching

"The kind of thing I'm good at is knowing every politician in the state and remembering where he itches. And I know where to scratch him."

> —Earl Long (three-term governor of Louisiana)

Baggage

"The next time anybody wants to know about Tawana Brawley, I'm going to ask them, 'Do you ask Teddy Kennedy about Chappaquiddick? Do you ask Hillary Clinton about her husband?'"

> —Al Sharpton (2004 presidential candidate)

Base Closings

"We will not close any bases that are not needed."

> —Les Aspin (secretary of defense, 1993–1994)

 Lloyd Bentsen

"The senator from Texaco."

> —Ernest Hollings (senator from South
> Carolina, 1965–2004), on then–Texas
> Democratic Senator Lloyd Bentsen, a
> supporter of the oil and gas industry

Best and the Brightest

"They may be just as intelligent as you say. But I'd
feel a helluva lot better if just one of them had ever
run for sheriff."

> —Lyndon Johnson (president, 1963–1969),
> on high-powered advisers to President
> John Kennedy

Bimbo Eruptions

"Who is going to find out? These women are trash.
Nobody's going to believe them."

> —Hillary Rodham Clinton (first lady,
> 1993–2001), on her husband's affairs

★ Bipartisanship

"I don't like bipartisans. Whenever a fellow tells me he's bipartisan, I know that he's going to vote against me."

—Harry Truman (president, 1945–1953)

★ Black Vote

"It was the black vote that decided the 2000 election—Clarence Thomas'."

—Carol Moseley Braun (2004 presidential candidate)

★ Boats

"I wanted to have *Playboy* bunnies come on at night to meet with me. I wanted to be promiscuous with them."

— James Traficant (representative from Ohio, 1985–2002), explaining why he kept a boat docked in the Potomac River

🐴 Boobs

"I think it's about time we voted for senators with breasts. After all, we've been voting for boobs long enough."

> —Clarie Sargent (senatorial candidate from Arizona in 1992)

🐴 Boring

"All I really want is to be boring. When people talk about me, I'd like them to say, 'Carol's basically a short Bill Bradley.' Or: 'Carol's kind of like Al Gore in a skirt.'"

> —Carol Moseley Braun (senator from Illinois, 1993–1998), in 1993

🐴 Brain Levels

"Maybe it's at a level my brain can't reach."

> —Zell Miller (senator from Georgia, 1999–2004), on Democratic criticism of President Bush's tax cut

🫏 Bras

"Madame Speaker, it started with the training bra and then it came to the push-up bra. The support bra, the Wonderbra, the super bra. It is called the holster bra, the gun bra. That is right, a brassiere to conceal a hidden handgun. Unbelievable. What is next? A maxi-girdle to conceal a stinger missile? Beam me up. I advise all men in America against taking women to drive-in movies who may end up getting shot in a passionate embrace. I yield back all those plain old Maidenform brassieres and chainlink pantyhouse."

— James Traficant

🫏 Carol Moseley Braun

"This so boggles the mind that one wonders whether we ought to be instituting some mental competency test to people before they announce they're running for president."

—Gerald Austin (political consultant), on Carol Moseley Braun running for president

🫏 Bravery

"Are you big enough to make me, you, you little wimp? . . . I dare you, you little fruitcake!"

> —Fortney Pete Stark (congressman from California, 1973–), after having been told to "shut up" by Colorado Republican Congressman Scott McInnis

"I'm an elderly gentleman. I haven't been in a fight involving bodily contact in sixty years. Look, I fall trying to put on my underwear in the morning."

> —Fortney Pete Stark, denying that he threatened another member of Congress with physical violence

🫏 Brushes

"People say I've had brushes with the law. That's not true. I've had brushes with overzealous prosecutors."

> —Edwin Edwards (four-term governor of Louisiana), on his twelfth grand jury probe in a decade

★ Budget Deficit

"If it were a movie, it would be *Honey, I Shrunk the Surplus.*"

> —Hillary Rodham Clinton (senator from New York, 2001–), on George W. Bush's handling of the federal budget

★ Bumper Sticker

VOTE FOR THE CROOK. IT'S IMPORTANT.

> —bumper sticker for Edwin Edwards, in his 1991 campaign against David Duke for governor of Louisiana

★ Bureaucrats

"A bureaucrat is a Democrat who holds some office that a Republican wants."

> —Harry Truman (president, 1945–1953)

"I will break out of prison and I'll make a neck tie out of some of these bureaucrats."

> —James Traficant (representative from Ohio, 1985–2002), on his post-prison plans

🫏 Burglary

"The Democratic Party, all the candidates from Washington, they all know each other, they all move in the same circles, and what I'm doing is breaking into the country club."

> —Howard Dean (2004 presidential candidate), several days after his seventeen-year-old son was arrested for breaking into a country club

🫏 George W. Bush

"The difference between Martin Sheen and George W. Bush is Martin Sheen is actually convincing when he acts like he's the president."

> —Paul Begala (Clinton White House staffer)

"He deserves a one-way bus ticket back to Crawford, Texas."

> —Howard Dean (2004 presidential candidate)

"You can't find a better fraternity brother."

> —Ernest Hollings (senator from South Carolina, 1965–2004)

"They elected the symbol of ebonics to the presidency of this nation. There ain't no brother in Oakland, or anywhere else, that would run the phrases or mix up the words the way this cat does. It raises questions about whether he's really white."

> —Willie Brown (mayor of San Francisco, 1996–2004)

"He's as confounded as he is confused. He's as flummoxed as he is floundering. He's as puzzled as he is perplexed."

> —Chris Lehane (press secretary, Gore for President campaign)

"The poor boy just campaigns all the time. He pays no attention to what's going on in Congress."

> —Ernest Hollings

"All over the country people are asking whether or not George Bush is smart enough to be president of the United States. And the scary thing is, one of the people asking me was Dan Quayle."

> —John Kerry (2004 presidential candidate)

"We have a president who thinks foreign territory is the opponent's dugout and Kashmir is a sweater."

> —Fortney Pete Stark (representative from California, 1973–)

"Like father, like son: Four years and he's done."

> —Dick Gephardt (2004 presidential candidate)

"The Bush operation reminds me of North Korea. You have a group of insanely loyal, fiercely committed fanatics, devoting their lives to slavish devotion of a moron whose only claim to power is that his father used to run the country. George W. Bush is Kim Jong II with better hair."

> —Paul Begala (Clinton White House staffer)

"This is a guy who could not find oil in Texas."

> —Al Franken (Democratic activist and humorist)

🫏 Bushes

"There's more with Gore! Stay out of the Bushes!"

> —Jesse Jackson (1988 presidential candidate), in a frequent refrain during the 2000 presidential campaign

🐴 Bushonomics

"His economic plan could fit on the back of a shampoo bottle: cut taxes, increase spending, borrow, repeat."

> —Joe Lieberman (2004 presidential candidate), on President George W. Bush

🐴 Cactus

"I have learned the difference between a cactus and a caucus. On a cactus, the pricks are on the outside."

> —Morris Udall (representative from Arizona, 1961–1992)

🐴 California

"California is the most progressive state in the nation. I don't think anyone here will have a problem with a smut peddler as governor."

> —Larry Flynt (2003 California gubernatorial candidate)

"I'm not one of the loons."

> —Ronald Palmieri (Los Angeles attorney running for governor of California in the 2003 recall election)

"All over the country, it's hurting our reputation and we need to get it over with. It's all my A.G. colleagues talk about, is what a *Gong Show* we are in California."

> —Bill Lockyer (attorney general of California, 1999–)

"A coup attempt by the Taliban element of the California Republican Party."

> —Bob Mulholland (political director, California Democratic Party), on the 2003 California recall election

"The recall petition would be handed to that Republican at their swearing-in, absolutely."

> —Bob Mulholland, on the likelihood that California Democrats would initiate a recall election if Governor Gray Davis was replaced by a Republican

🐴 Cameras

"If you don't get those cameras out of my face, I'm gonna go 8.6 on the Richter scale with gastric emissions that'll clear this room!"

> —James Traficant (representative from Ohio, 1985–2002), to photographers covering his House ethics hearing

🐴 Campaigning

"It's either one of the best things I've ever done or one of the dumbest."

> —Janet Reno (U.S. attorney general, 1993–2001), on running for governor of Florida in 2002

"If you have thirty cousins, it's pretty easy."

> —Joseph Kennedy, Jr. (representative from Massachusetts, 1987–1998), when asked about the difficulties of campaign fundraising

"[Non-candidates] don't have to do what the candidates do—talk about huge issues in thirty seconds in a field somewhere, trying to make sure cows don't urinate on our shoes."

> —Mario Cuomo (governor of New York, 1983–1994)

Capitalism

"This is capitalism. You invest in a stock; it goes up, it goes down."

> —Terry McAuliffe (chairman, Democratic National Committee), on making $18 million from a $100,000 sweetheart investment in Global Crossing, the telecommunications giant that went bankrupt

Car Honking

"Oh, that was you?"

> —Hillary Rodham Clinton (senator from New York, 2001–), to David Letterman on *The Late Show*. Letterman lives near the Clintons' residence in Chappaqua, New York. He said, "Every idiot in the area is going to drive by honking now."

🐴 Carpetbagging

"I'm for anybody from Chicago coming to New York."

> —Hillary Rodham Clinton, on the possible trade of Chicago Cubs slugger Sammy Sosa to the New York Yankees

🐴 Caution

"Beware of Greeks bearing gifts, colored men looking for loans, and whites who 'understand the Negro.'"

> —Adam Clayton Powell (representative from New York, 1945–1970)

🐴 Lincoln Chafee

"Now when I hear someone talking about a Rhode Island politician whose father was a senator and who got to Washington on his family name, used cocaine, and wasn't very smart, I know there is only a fifty-fifty chance it's me."

> —Patrick Kennedy (representative from Rhode Island, 1995–), joking about Rhode Island Republican Senator Lincoln Chafee at a roast

🐴 Chauvinism

"I am not a chauvinist, obviously. . . . I believe in women's rights for every woman but my own."

—Harold Washington (mayor of Chicago, 1983–1987)

🐴 Chicago Cubs

"Being a Cubs fan prepares you for life—and Washington."

—Hillary Rodham Clinton

🐴 Chinese Fundraising Scandal

"Mistakes were made . . ."

—Bill Clinton (president 1993–2001), admitting that he and the Democratic National Committee continued to "raise money on the promise of guaranteeing specific kinds of access"

🐴 Choices

"My choice early in life was either to be a piano player in a whorehouse or a politician. And to tell the truth, there's hardly any difference."

—Harry Truman (president, 1945–1953)

🫏 Christians

"I think people don't care so much where he [Lieberman] goes to church on Sunday, but just that he has the moral values and principles to lead this country."

> —John Breaux (senator from Louisiana, 1987–2004)

🫏 Christmas

"Mr. Speaker, the school prayer issue is out of control, literally. Students in Pennsylvania were prohibited from handing out Christmas cards. Reports say students in Minnesota were disciplined for having said 'Merry Christmas.' Now if that is not enough to find coal in your athletic supporter, check this out: A school board in Georgia removed the word *Christmas* from their school calendar because the ACLU threatened to sue. Beam me up. If this is religious freedom, I am a fashion model for *GQ*."

> —James Traficant (representative from Ohio, 1985–2002)

"I didn't wake up like it was Christmas morning and say, 'Oh, my gosh, did I get my pardon?'"

> —Roger Clinton (brother of President Clinton), concerned that some of his friends did not receive last-minute pardons from his brother

"Christmas is a time when kids tell Santa what they want, and adults pay for it. Deficits are when adults tell the government what they want—and their kids pay for it."

> —Richard Lamm (governor of Colorado, 1975–1986)

🐴 CIA

"The CIA is made up of boys whose families sent them to Princeton but wouldn't let them in the family brokerage business."

> —Lyndon Johnson (president, 1963–1969)

🐴 Bill Clinton

"My daddy talks on the telephone, drinks coffee, and makes 'peeches."

> —Chelsea Clinton (daughter of Bill Clinton), at age four

"President Clinton didn't start out with a lot of scrupolousity."

> —Jerry Brown (mayor of Oakland, 1998–)

"He almost makes Nixon look like a moral giant."

> —Tom Finneran (speaker, Massachusetts House of Representatives, 1996–)

"He has a detective shit-detector about personal relationships sometimes. He is also careless about his appearance."

> —Betsey Wright (longtime assistant to President Clinton)

"Clinton's about as popular as AIDS in South Carolina."

> —Ernest Hollings (senator from South Carolina, 1965–2004)

"He's like the guy you don't want your child to go out with."

> —Gene Taylor (representative from Mississippi, 1989–)

"If you allow him to drive the golf cart, he'll run straight into a tree."

> —Webster Hubbell (assistant attorney general, 1993–1994), on *Politically Incorrect*

"If I didn't kick his ass every day, he wouldn't be worth anything."

> —Hillary Rodham Clinton (first lady, 1993–2001)

⭐ Hillary Rodham Clinton

"She is strong as garlic in a milkshake."

> —Paul Begala (Clinton White House staffer)

"The first lady is sorry she can't be with you tonight. If you believe that, I've got some land in Arkansas I'd like to sell you."

> —Bill Clinton (president 1993–2001), joking at the Gridiron Dinner in Washington in March 1995

"Hillary Clinton, the next junior senator from New York, and, of course, her lovely husband, Bill."

> —Ann Richards (governor of Texas, 1991–1994), introducing Hillary and Bill Clinton at a fundraising dinner in Washington, D.C., in June 1999

"I did think it was effective when I weaved in stories of real people in the audience and their everyday challenges. Like the woman here tonight whose husband is about to lose his job. She is struggling to get out of public housing and get a job on her own. Hillary Clinton, I want to fight for you!"

> —Al Gore (vice president 1993–2001), joking at the Al Smith dinner in 2000

"Buy one, get one free."

> —Bill Clinton, during the 1992 presidential campaign. Hillary often chimed in, "People call us two-for-one. The blue light special."

🐴 Cloakrooms

"You've got to work things out in the cloakroom, and when you've got them worked out, you can debate a little before you vote."

> —Lyndon Johnson (president 1963–1969)

🐴 Cockfighting

"This is not about cockfighting. It's about the proper role of the federal government. . . . John Locke, Montesquieu, and Patrick Henry would have said to leave policing chickens to state and local governments, and I do, too."

> —Zell Miller (senator from Georgia, 1999–2004), opposing Congressional legislation to ban the transport of live chickens across state lines for cockfighting

🐴 Cockpit Security

"Just keep the cockpit door closed. You can put up a sign in Arab—that is, say, typecasting, but say, 'Try to hijack, go to jail.'"

> —Ernest Hollings (senator from South Carolina, 1965–2004)

🐴 Commonalities

"Like many of us, I grew up in a small town in North Carolina."

> —John Edwards (2004 presidential candidate), in a speech to the California Democratic Party convention in 2002

🐴 Computers

"I'm not an expert on computers."

> —Al Gore (vice president 1993–2001), asked how his subpeoned White House e-mails got lost

🐴 Conditions

"When we got into office, the thing that surprised me the most was that things were as bad as we'd been saying they were."

> —John Kennedy (president, 1961–1963)

🐴 Confederate Heroes

"I want people to see that if I'll go to Robert E. Lee's tomb, I'll go anywhere. I wonder how this will play in Harlem."

> —Al Sharpton (2004 presidential candidate)

🫏 Confidence

"[I could not lose unless I was] caught in bed with a dead girl or a live boy."

> —Edwin Edwards (four-term governor of Louisiana), on his 1983 gubernatorial campaign

🫏 Confirmation

"I'm confirmed; I'm not looking for a job. I'm all loosey-goosey now."

> —Donna Shalala (secretary of health and human services, 1993–2001)

🫏 Congress

"Making Congress look even sillier than it sometimes looks would not be high on my priority list."

> —Barney Frank (representative from Massachusetts, 1981–), on the decision to replace "French fries" with "freedom fries" in the House cafeteria

⭐ Congressmen

"Give a member of Congress a junket and a mimeograph machine and he thinks he is secretary of state."

> —Dean Rusk (secretary of state, 1961–1969)

"I've had a tough time learning to be a congressman. Today I accidentally spent some of my own money."

> —Joseph Kennedy, Jr. (representative from Massachusetts, 1987–1998)

⭐ Conservatives

"A conservative is a man with two perfectly good legs who, however, has never learned how to walk forward."

> —Franklin Delano Roosevelt (president, 1933–1945)

⭐ Consistency

"The position I'm taking now is an expansion, not a reversal."

> —Dennis Kucinich (2004 presidential candidate), explaining his changed position on abortion, from pro-life to pro-choice

🐴 Co-Presidency

"I'm not going to have some reporters pawing through our papers. We are the president."

> —Hillary Rodham Clinton (first lady, 1993–2001), discussing possible release of Whitewater documents

🐴 Consciousness

"In our soul's magnificence, we become conscious of the cosmos within us. We hear the music of peace, we hear the music of cooperation, we hear the music of love. In our soul's forgetting, we become unconscious of our cosmic birthright, blighted with disharmony, disunity, torn asunder from the stars in a disaster."

> —Dennis Kucinich

🐴 Conservatives

"A conservative is someone who makes no changes and consults his grandmother when in doubt."

> —Woodrow Wilson (president, 1913–1921)

"If this were Germany, we would call it fascism. If this were South Africa, we would call it racism. Here we call it conservatism."

> —Jesse Jackson (1988 presidential candidate). Jackson went on to compare the Christian Coalition to the Nazi SS and Southern slave owners.

Constitution

"The last time I checked, the Constitution said, 'Of the people, by the people, and for the people.' That's what the Declaration of Independence says."

> —Bill Clinton (president, 1993–2001), quoting from Abraham Lincoln's Gettysburg Address

"Due to a small but significant clause in the U.S. Constitution, I will be out of the office from January 21, 2001 until January 20, 2005."

> —Michael Feldman (adviser to Vice President Gore), on his White House voice-mail message

🐴 Contract with America

"When I compare this to what happened in Germany, I hope that you will see the similarities to what is happening to us."

> —Charles Rangel (representative from New York, 1971–)

"These are people who are practicing genocide with a smile; they're worse than Hitler."

> —Major Owens (representative from New York, 1983–)

🐴 Cooperation

"If you can't think of anything to say, just implement my vision."

> —Gray Davis (governor of California, 1999–2003), speaking to fifteen California state legislators before they addressed a political gathering concerning public transportation

🫏 Corruption

"I think because he could not say *nigger*, he said the word *corrupt*."

> —Carol Moseley Braun (senator from Illinois, 1993–1998), during her 1998 reelection campaign, responding to a column by George Will summarizing the corruption charges against her. Braun also said, "George Will can take his hood and go back to wherever he came from." The next day, she apologized.

🫏 Coxswain

"Hey! Look at this—I'm a cocks'n! Does my wife know?"

> —John Breaux (senator from Louisiana, 1987–2004), upon being named an honorary "coxswain" of the U.S. Coast Guard. Passing a Hooters restaurant, Breaux cracked, "Hey! Maybe I should get a job there, since I'm a cocks'n!"

★ Crack

"This bill is the legislative equivalent of crack. It yields a short-term high but does long-term damage to the system and it's expensive to boot."

> —Barney Frank (representative from
> Massachusetts, 1981–)

★ Jim Crow

"We have defeated Jim Crow, but now we have to deal with his son, James Crow, Jr., Esquire."

> —Al Sharpton (2004 presidential candidate)

★ Mario Cuomo

"[Mario Cuomo is a] mean son of a bitch who acts like a mafioso."

> —Bill Clinton (president, 1993–2001), on
> the telephone with Gennifer Flowers

 **Currency**

"Currency per se is not illegal. . . . The federal government prints cash every day."

> —Edwin Edwards (four-time governor of Louisiana), after the FBI seized $400,000 in cash from his safety-deposit box. The FBI claimed that Edwards, while governor of Louisiana, extorted the money from Eddie DeBartolo, owner of the San Francisco 49ers, as a bribe for a casino license.

🐴 Dade County

"Voting in Dade County is a lot like going to a casino. You hope it will work out, but you know it's beyond your control."

> —Carrie Meek (representative from Florida, 1993–), on voting machine problems that plagued the 2002 Florida primaries

🐴 Dairy Farming

"I'm very familiar with the importance of dairy farming in Wisconsin. I've spent the night on a dairy farm here in Wisconsin. If I'm entrusted with the presidency, you'll have someone who is very familiar with what the Wisconsin dairy industry is all about."

> —Al Gore during the 2000 presidential campaign

🐴 *The Dating Game*

"It's not *The Dating Game*. . . . You don't have to fall in love with Al Gore; I did that."

> —Tipper Gore (wife of Al Gore), during the 2000 presidential campaign

"Who wants a boring governor, anyway?"

>—Jennifer Granholm (governor of Michigan, 2003–), asked about her appearance on *The Dating Game* in 1979

Gray Davis

"I may be his only friend."

>—Willie Brown (mayor of San Francisco, 1996–2004), on Gray Davis, the governor of California

"I might be paralyzed from the waist down, but unlike Gray Davis, I'm not paralyzed from the neck up."

>—Larry Flynt (2003 California gubernatorial candidate)

"This may be the first time the words *Gray Davis* and *electricity* have ever appeared in the same sentence."

>—Gray Davis (governor of California, 1999–2003), on his image and the California energy crisis

🫏 Deals

"I'd like to start by offering you a deal, Jack. If you don't use any old football stories, I won't tell any of my warm and humorous stories about chlorofluorocarbon abatement."

> —Al Gore, during his 1996 vice presidential debate with Jack Kemp

🫏 Howard Dean

"You've been saying for many months that you're the head of the Democratic wing of the Democratic Party. I think you're just winging it."

> —Dick Gephardt (2004 presidential candidate), to Howard Dean in a debate

"Ultimately, voters are going to decide a small-town physician from a small and atypical state is probably not qualified to lead this nation in a dangerous world."

> —Jim Jordan (manager, John Kerry for President campaign)

"You know, to listen to Senator Lieberman, Senator Kerry, Representative Gephardt, I'm anti-Israel, I'm anti-trade, I'm anti-Medicare, and I'm anti–Social Security. I wonder how I ended up in the Democratic Party."

> —Howard Dean (2004 presidential candidate)

★ Dear Diary

"11:15–11:20 Miami Lake townhouse kitchen—give Adele dry cleaning—newspapers—collect Coca Cola."

> —Bob Graham (2004 presidential candidate), in an excerpt from the minute-by-minute logs he has kept for more than twenty-five years

★ Debates

"Our debates have been like the mating of pandas in the zoo—the expectations are high, there's a lot of fuss and commotion, but there's never any kind of result."

> —Bruce Babbitt (1988 presidential candidate)

"We're too old for *Survivor* and *Star Search*."

> —Bill Clinton (president, 1993–2001), explaining why he and Bob Dole signed a contract to debate national issues on *60 Minutes*

🫏 Decisions

"I make my decisions horizontally, not vertically."

> —Bob Kerrey (senator from Nebraska, 1989–2000)

🫏 Defeat

"If I lose, I'm going to retire from politics, practice law, and wear bright leather pants."

> —Carol Moseley Braun (senator from Illinois, 1993–1998)

🫏 Democratic Leadership Council

"The [Democratic Leadership Council] was led by folks like Bill Clinton, Al Gore, and Joe Lieberman and was set up as the anti–Rainbow Coalition . . . I am running to take out the Democratic Leadership Council, which I call the Democratic Leisure Class, because that's who it serves—the leisure class and the wealthy."

> —Al Sharpton (2004 presidential candidate)

🐴 Democratic Party

"Once upon a time, the most successful Democratic leader of them all, FDR, looked south and said, 'I see one-third of a nation ill-housed, ill-clad, ill-nourished.' Today, our national Democratic leaders look south and say, 'I see one-third of a nation and it can go to hell.'"

> —Zell Miller (senator from Georgia, 1999–2004) from his book, *A National Party No More: The Conscience of a Conservative Democrat*

"Assisted suicide."

> —Evan Bayh (senator from Indiana, 1999–), asked whether the woes of the Democratic Party were the result of Democratic mistakes or Republican attacks

🐴 Departing

"If I had known how much packing I'd have to do, I'd have run again."

> —Harry Truman (president, 1945–1953), on leaving the White House

 Differences

"Am I different? Yeah. Deep down, you know you want to wear wider bottoms; you're just not secure enough. . . . Do I do my hair with a weed whacker? I admit it."

> —James Traficant (representative from Ohio, 1985—2002), in his farewell speech to the House on July 24, 2002

Dignity

"I'm sure this is funny. But at the end of this, I want to have some bread crumbs leading back to my dignity."

> —Al Gore (2000 presidential candidate), expressing objections to a sketch about flatulence during rehearsal for his appearance on *Saturday Night Live* in December 2002

Disparagement

"I will not have any disparaging remarks about him except I hate him."

> —William Donald Schaefer (governor of Maryland, 1987–1995), on his successor, Parris Glendening

🐴 Distinctiveness

"It doesn't matter what I say as long as I sound different from other politicians."

> —Jerry Brown (governor of California, 1975–1983)

🐴 Diversity

"How do they define diversity? Having two guys to lead the ticket from two different oil companies?"

> —Rob Reiner (Gore campaign adviser), on the Bush-Cheney ticket

🐴 Division

"Have you ever tried to split sawdust?"

> —Eugene McCarthy (senator from Minnesota, 1959–1970), asked in 1969 whether he had divided the Democratic Party by running against President Johnson in 1968

ᴤ Dixie

"Rather I should die a thousand times, and see Old Glory trampled in the dirt never to rise again, than to see this beloved land of ours become degraded by race mongrels, a throwback to the blackest specimen from the wilds."

> —Robert Byrd (senator from West Virginia, 1959–), in a 1944 letter (a year after he left the Ku Klux Klan)

ᴤ Donations

"A check or credit card, a Gucci bag strap, anything of value will do. Give as you live."

> —Jesse Jackson (1988 presidential candidate), at a fundraising event in Aspen, Colorado

ᴤ Doughnuts

"As a free man, I take pride in the words '*Ich bin ein Berliner.*'"

> —John Kennedy (president, 1961–1963), near the Berlin Wall in 1963. The German translation is "I am a small jam doughnut." He meant to say, "*Ich bin Berliner.*"

🐴 Draft

"Thank you for saving me from the draft."

> —Bill Clinton (president, 1993–2001), in a 1969 letter to retired U.S. Army ROTC Colonel Eugene Holmes, chairman of Clinton's local draft board

🐴 Driving

"If you want to go forward, you put it in D, and if you want to go in reverse, you put it in R."

> —Timothy Kaine (lieutenant governor of Virginia, 2001–), using a line during the 2001 election that many Democratic candidates have used on the campaign trail

"Well, I think Dad learned a lot."

> —Chelsea Clinton, at age sixteen, asked about getting a driving lesson from her father at Camp David

🐎 David Duke

"We're both wizards under the sheets."

> —Edwin Edwards (four-term governor of Louisiana), asked by a reporter during the 1991 gubernatorial race, "What do you and David Duke have in common?" (David Duke was a grand wizard in the Ku Klux Klan.)

🐎 Earrings

"If God wanted you to wear earrings, he'd have made you a girl."

> —Don Siegelman (governor of Alabama, 1999–2003), on a local school board policy banning earrings on boys

🐎 Earth

"I just had to call, because you've printed a picture of the Earth upside down in the front page of the paper."

> —Al Gore, in a 1988 phone conversation with an editor at *The Washington Post*

"We have probed the earth, excavated it, burned it, ripped things from it, buried things in it. . . . That does not fit my definition of a good tenant. If we were here on a month-to-month basis, we would have been evicted long ago."

>—Rose Bird (chief justice, California Supreme Court, 1977–1986)

🐴 Economists

"I listen to what these propeller-heads have to say, and then I go ahead and say that I am for a tax cut."

>—Zell Miller (senator from Georgia, 1999–2004), on economists who said that president Bush's tax cut plan was too generous

🐴 Economy

"I'm glad the president finally found an economic development program. I'm just sad that it's only in Baghdad."

>—John Kerry (2004 presidential candidate), during a Democratic presidential candidates debate

"Senator Clinton said this was the worst administration in economics since Herbert Hoover. I think that's defaming the Hoover family."

> —James Carville (political consultant), on *Meet the Press*

⭐ John Edwards

"A Ken doll is plastic, lacking in substance, and can be bought for about ten dollars. There's at least one critical difference right there."

> —John Edwards (2004 presidential candidate), joking at the Gridiron Club dinner, challenging a columnist's contention that he was little more than a Ken doll

⭐ Elections

"I stand here with the true understanding and knowledge that it is the Lord who decides elections."

> —Ed Rendell (governor of Pennsylvania, 2003–), campaigning in a church two days before Pennsylvania's Democratic gubernatorial primary in 2002

🫏 Elvis

"Trouble was, Elvis was usually pretty loaded when he called."

> —Hamilton Jordan (President Carter's White House chief of staff, 1977–1981), on Elvis Presley's frequent calls to the White House

🫏 Embarrassment

"The only thing I'm embarrassed about is, I have to explain to my two teenage daughters why I wore such a cheap cowboy hat."

> —Al Sharpton (2004 presidential candidate), asked whether he had any remorse about a federal surveillance tape showing him discussing a drug deal with an FBI undercover agent

🫏 Employment

"What do we want our kids to do? Sweep around Japanese computers?"

> —Walter Mondale (vice president, 1977–1981), in a 1982 speech to an electrical workers union

★ Environmentalists

"I know they are environmentalists. I heard a lot of my speeches recycled."

> —Jesse Jackson (1988 presidential candidate), on the 1992 Democratic presidential field

★ Equality

"I always had a very vivid and clear sense that men and women were entirely and completely equal—if not more so."

> —Al Gore (vice president, 1993–2001), before a women's political group in 1999

★ Evasion

"That's a good question. Let me try to evade you."

> —Paul Tsongas (1992 presidential candidate)

★ Executions

"I'd have to think about it."

> —Al Gore, asked on *Meet the Press* if he would favor postponing the execution of a pregnant woman

False Rumors

"Don't believe any false rumors unless you hear them from me."

> —Vic Schiro (mayor of New Orleans, 1961–1970)

Jerry Falwell

"I wouldn't piss down that son of a bitch's throat if his heart was on fire."

> —James Carville (political consultant)

Family Business

"I've got one politician in the family, and that's enough."

> —Bill Clinton, on the possibilty that he might run for mayor of New York City

🐴 Family Secrets

"We've uncovered some embarrassing ancestors in the not-too-distant past. Some horse thieves, and some people killed on Saturday nights. One of my relatives, unfortunately, was even in the newspaper business."

> —Jimmy Carter (president, 1977–1981)

🐴 Favoritism

"There are no favorites in my office. I treat them all with the same general inconsideration."

> —Lyndon Johnson (president, 1963–1969)

🐴 Five-Letter Words

"I would not use the three-letter word. I would use the five-letter word: deceit."

> —Bob Graham (2004 presidential candidate), asked at the NAACP annual convention if President Bush had told a lie about Iraq's efforts to purchase uranium in Africa

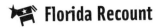 Florida Recount

"You don't have to get snippy about it."

> —Al Gore to George W. Bush on election
> night 2000, withdrawing his previous
> concession. Bush had said, "Let me make
> sure that I understand. You're calling
> back to retract that concession?"

"Let me explain something to you. Your brother is
not the ultimate authority on this."

> —Al Gore to George W. Bush on election
> night 2000. Bush had said that his
> brother, Florida Governor Jeb Bush,
> affirmed that he had carried Florida.

Gennifer Flowers

"We have to destroy her."

> —Hillary Rodham Clinton (first lady,
> 1993–2001) during the 1992 presidential
> campaign, on Gennifer Flowers, who
> stated that she'd had a twelve-year affair
> with Bill Clinton

⭐ Jerry Ford

"Jerry Ford is so dumb he can't fart and chew gum at the same time."

—Lyndon Johnson

⭐ Foreign Leaders

"But not knowing the names . . . I think that's kind of understandable. I mean, the other day I was talking to Otkir Sultonov. You know, the prime minister of Uzbekistan. And he asked me, 'Did you send a birthday card to Hamed?' That's of course Hamed Karoui, the prime minister of Tunisia. I had just been talking about him with Ion Sturza, the prime minister of Moldova. We're old friends. We actually met through a mutual friend, Lennart Meri, the president of Estonia, of course."

—Al Gore, joking on the Don Imus radio show about the fact that, in 1999, George W. Bush could not name the leaders of Taiwan, India, Pakistan, or Chechnya

🫏 Forgiveness

"In the Bible it says they asked Jesus how many times we should forgive, and he said seventy times seven. Well, I want you to know that I'm keeping a chart."

> —Hillary Rodham Clinton

"Forgive your enemies, but never forget their names."

> —John Kennedy (president, 1961–1963)

🫏 Freedom

"I don't have to get elected to a boomin' thing. And I don't have to do things that are politically correct. The hell with everybody. I'm free at last."

> —Ernest Hollings (senator from South Carolina, 1965–2004), on election eve 1992, when he apparently thought he would be defeated for reelection. Hollings won the 1992 election, and was reelected again in 1998.

🐴 Friends

"I've always said that in politics, your enemies can't hurt you, but your friends will kill you."

>—Ann Richards (governor of Texas, 1991–1994)

🐴 Fundraising

"With this fundraising being successful as it is, as God is my witness, I will not go hungry again."

>—Carol Moseley Braun (senator from Illinois, 1993–1998)

🐴 Futurama

"I think I may have a future as a disembodied head."

>—Al Gore, commenting on his appearance on the TV show *Futurama*

🐴 Fuzzy Math

"I'd like to say I'm forty-three, but that's fuzzy math."

>—Hillary Rodham Clinton, on her fifty-third birthday

🐴 Gay Marriage

"That's like asking me, 'Do I support black marriage, or white marriage?'"

> —Al Sharpton (presidential candidate, 2004), at a candidates' forum sponsored by the Human Rights Campaign

🐴 Getting Down

"Motown, Motown: That's my era. Those are my people."

> —Hillary Rodham Clinton (senator from New York, 2001–), during an interview in 2000 with Hot 97, a Manhattan hip-hop radio station

🐴 Newt Gingrich

"I almost feel sorry for Newt Gingrich. President Clinton has an affair with a twenty-one-year-old, and [Gingrich] loses his job."

> —George Stephanopoulos (Clinton White House staffer), after the November 1998 elections

⭐ Giraffes

"I have been working in a male culture for a very long time, and I haven't met the first one who wants to go out and hunt a giraffe."

> —Pat Schroeder (representative from Colorado, 1973–1996), in 1995, responding to then–House Speaker Newt Gingrich's statement that "males are biologically driven to go out and hunt giraffes"

⭐ Rudy Giuliani

"His wife kicked him out, and he moved in with two gay men and a Shih Tzu. Is that South Carolina values? I don't think so."

> —Alex Sanders (2002 senatorial candidate from South Carolina). Giuliani came to South Carolina to campaign for the Republican nominee, Lindsay Graham.

"We would have come together if Bozo was the mayor."

> —Al Sharpton (2004 presidential candidate), on Rudy Giuliani's leadership after September 11

"Now I know why he likes opera."

> —Hillary Rodham Clinton (senator from New York, 2001–), on Rudy Guliani's storied personal life

⭐ Gladiator

"And then when I get out, I will grab a sword like Maximus Demidius and as a gladiator I will stab people in the crotch."

> —James Traficant (representative from Ohio, 1985–2002), talking about his plans once he is released from prison. Maximus Demidius was Russell Crowe's character in the film *Gladiator*.

⭐ Good Government

"I've had just about all of this good-government stuff I can stand."

> —Charles Jones (Louisiana state senator, 1992–)

"I'm for pretty good government."

> —Gillis Long (representative from Louisiana, 1963–1964, 1973–1986). Gillis Long is Huey Long's cousin.

🐴 Good Points

"You had some good points you brought up. It was kinda long, so I forgot some of them."

> —Diana Bajoie (Louisiana state senator, 1991–), during debate in the Senate Health and Welfare Committee

🐴 Al Gore

"I lost weight and shaved a beard. He gained weight and grew a beard."

> —Al Sharpton (2004 Democratic presidential candidate), contrasting his preparation for the 2004 presidential campaign to Al Gore's

"I'm changing the subject real quickly here."

> —Christopher Dodd (senator from Connecticut, 1981–), asked to assess Al Gore's chances if he ran for president in 2004

🐴 Greatness

"This is still the greatest country in the world, if we just will steel our wills and lose our minds."

> —Bill Clinton (president, 1993–2001), at the University of Florida in 1992

⭐ Lani Guinier

"The theories—the ideas she expressed about equality of results with legislative bodies and with—by outcome, by decisions made by legislative bodies, ideas related to proportional voting as a general remedy, not in particular cases where the circumstances make that a feasible idea."

> —Al Gore (vice president, 1993–2001), on *Nightline*, defending President Clinton's decision to withdraw the nomination of Lani Guinier to be assistant attorney general for civil rights because of her views on proportional representation

⭐ Katherine Harris

"She doesn't know election law. She couldn't even resign properly."

> —Bob Poe (chairman of the Florida Demo-
> cratic Party), on the retroactive resigna-
> tion of Katherine Harris, Florida's
> secretary of state. Harris was required by
> state
> election laws—which she administered—
> to resign on July 15, 2002, the day she
> became legally eligible in her race for
> Congress. She did not resign until
> August 1.

⭐ Head Busting

"If you like Governor Foster, vote for it. If you dis-
like Governor Foster, vote for it so he can go down
the road and bust his head wide open."

> —Juba Diez (Louisiana state representative,
> 1975–), urging the Louisiana House to
> pass a bill supported by the governor to
> allow motorcyclists to ride without
> helmets

 **Heart Surgery**

"It was a little like opening the hood of your car to change the spark plugs and doing a full tuneup."

> —Bob Graham (2004 presidential candidate), joking that his heart surgery was more serious than he admitted initially

 **Heaven**

"It is possible to get to heaven in a Cadillac, but it is hard."

> —Mario Cuomo (governor of New York, 1983–1994)

 **Hell**

"I am in hell already. I am in Israel."

> —Al Sharpton, in 1991, responding to a Tel Aviv heckler who yelled, "Go to hell!"

🐴 Highest Court in the Land

"I didn't do this stuff. I will go all the way to the Supreme Court, The Hague, wherever they want to go."

> —Buddy Cianci (former mayor of Providence, Rhode Island), after a federal jury found him guilty of racketeering and conspiracy

🐴 Holistic View

"I have a holistic view of the world. I see the world as interconnected and interdependent and that leaves no room for war."

> —Dennis Kucinich (2004 presidential candidate)

🐴 Historians

"All the historians are Harvard people. It just isn't fair. Poor old Hoover from West Branch, Iowa, had no chance with that crowd; nor did Andrew Jackson from Tennessee. Nor does Lyndon Johnson from Stonewall, Texas. It just isn't fair."

> —Lyndon Johnson (president, 1963–1969)

Homelessness

"Speaking from my own religious tradition in this Christmas season, two thousand years ago a homeless woman gave birth to a homeless child in a manger because the inn was full."

>—Al Gore

Hookers

"I want to apologize to all the hookers in New York and Los Angeles for associating them with members of Congress."

>—James Traficant (representative from Ohio, 1985–2002). Traficant once referred to members of Congress as "prostitutes."

Hounddogging

"This is fun. Women are throwing themselves at me. All the while I was growing up, I was the fat boy in the Big Boy jeans."

>—Bill Clinton, while governor of Arkansas

🐴 Hurricanes

"All racial groups should be represented."

> —Sheila Jackson-Lee (representative from
> Texas, 1995–), asking the World Meteoro-
> logical Organization to give hurricanes
> such names as Keisha, Jamal, and
> Deshawn

🐴 Saddam Hussein

"After listening to you for an hour, I can tell that
you are a strong and intelligent man and that you
want peace."

> —Howard Metzenbaum (senator from Ohio,
> 1974–1994), in an April 1990 meeting
> with Saddam Hussein in Baghdad

"I suppose that's a good thing."

> —Howard Dean (2004 presidential
> candidate), on the fall of Saddam Hussein

🐴 Identity

"If you wake up in the morning and think you're white, you're going to meet someone before five o'clock who will let you know you're just another nigger."

> —Jesse Jackson (1988 presidential candidate)

🐴 Impeachment Trial

"To sit for seven hours and not talk is an unnatural act for a U.S. senator."

> —Max Cleland (senator from Georgia, 1997–2002), during the Clinton impeachment trial

🐴 Infidelity

"I've been married thirty-four years. I have not been a perfect man. I have made mistakes in my life."

> —Gary Condit (representative from California, 1989–2002), interviewed by Connie Chung about the disappearance of Chandra Levy. Condit repeated this phrase throughout the interview.

⭐ Insults

"I have been called a 'stupid and pathetic country bumpkin,' . . . compared to David Koresch, and blamed for a sixty-five point drop in the stock market, but never have I been called anything so repugnant . . . as a 'Washington Insider.'"

> —James Carville (political consultant)

⭐ Internal Revenue Service

"Madam Speaker, an investigation revealed that 16,000 IRS employees illegally used their computers. The report states that IRS agents spent 50 percent of their time at work on personal business. If that is not enough to service your revenue, IRS agents illegally used their computers for shopping, stock trading, gambling, and pornography. Unbelievable. Think about it. While 60 percent of taxpayer calls to the IRS go unanswered, the IRS agents were watching Marilyn Chambers do the Rotary International."

> —James Traficant (representative from Ohio, 1985–2002)

🐴 Internet

"Remember, America: I gave you the Internet, and I can take it away."

> —Al Gore (vice president, 1993–2001), joking on *Late Show with David Letterman* in 2000

🐴 Iraq

"Congress is not an ATM."

> —Robert Byrd (senator from West Virginia, 1959–), on President Bush's request for $87 billion in postwar assistance to Iraq

🐴 Israel

"If Iraq came across the Jordan River, I'd grab a rifle and fight and die for Israel."

> —Bill Clinton (president, 1993–2001), at a Zionist dinner in Toronto in July 2002

🫏 Jailhouse Rock

"The biggest obstacle was that he couldn't campaign. Other people had to do it for him."

> —Tish Traficant (wife of former Ohio Congressman James Traficant), on the problem her husband faced running for office from jail. Traficant is serving an eight-year prison sentence for bribery and racketeering. In 2002, while in prison, he received 27,000 votes for his old Congressional seat—15 percent of the vote.

🫏 Jews

"The Jews, I find, are very selfish."

> —Harry Truman (president, 1945–1953), in a recently discovered 1947 diary. Truman also said that Jews often expect "special treatment" and do not care about the suffering of other ethnic groups.

"If it were not for the strong support of the Jewish community for this war with Iraq, we would not be doing this. The leaders of the Jewish community are influential enough that they could change the direction of where this is going, and I think they should."

> —Jim Moran (representative from Virginia, 1991–). Moran was roundly criticized for this remark.

Jobs

"The president goes around the country speaking Spanish. The only Spanish he speaks when it comes to jobs is '*Hasta la vista.*'"

> —John Edwards (2004 presidential candidate), on George W. Bush's economic policies

Lyndon Johnson

"Hyperbole was to Lyndon Johnson what oxygen is to life."

> —Bill Moyers (press secretary to President Johnson)

🐴 Judicial Nominations

"They have an obligation to make sure that we're not getting a bunch of French figure skating judges."

> —Jack Quinn (White House counsel to President Clinton), on Senate Democrats' scrutiny of George W. Bush's judicial nominees

🐴 Jungle Bunnies

"I got jungle bunnies coming out of the woodwork to help Morial. It looks like Idi Amin has sent in troops."

> —Joe DiRosa (New Orleans mayoral candidate, 1978), commenting on supporters of his opponent, Dutch Morial

![donkey] Jack Kemp

"I think Jack Kemp just got into the passenger seat of the last scene of *Thelma and Louise*."

> —Bob Mulholland (political director, California Democratic Party), on Jack Kemp becoming Bob Dole's vice-presidential running mate in 1996

![donkey] John Kennedy

"Jack was out kissing babies while I was out passing bills. Someone had to tend the store."

> —Lyndon Johnson (vice president, 1961–1963), on John Kennedy winning the 1960 Democratic presidential nomination

"Senator, I served with Jack Kennedy. I knew Jack Kennedy. Jack Kennedy was a friend of mine. Senator, you're no Jack Kennedy."

> —Lloyd Bentsen (1988 vice presidential candidate), in his debate with Dan Quayle

🐴 John Kerry

"I wish he'd say to my face what he says behind my back."

> —Howard Dean (2004 presidential candidate), referring to Senator John Kerry. Moments before, Dean said, "I do have a mouth on me—that is, I generally say what I think, so I get in trouble."

🐴 King's English

"If the King's English was good enough for Jesus, it's good enough for me!"

> —Ma Ferguson (governor of Texas, 1925–1927, 1933–1935)

🐴 Lyndon LaRouche

"I suspect he's in jail."

> —Howard Dean (2004 presidential candidate), responding to shouts of "Where is LaRouche?" at the Congressional Black Caucus presidential debate in September 2003

🐴 Lavish Spending

"I have to borrow money from her to get a soft drink."

> —Jesse Jackson (1988 presidential candidate), responding to charges that he lives lavishly. He claimed that his wife controlled the family budget.

🐴 Kenneth Lay

"I did not have political relations with that man, Ken Lay."

> —Ernest Hollings (senator from South Carolina, 1965–2004), poking fun at George W. Bush's strategy of distancing himself from Enron chairman Kenneth Lay

🐴 Layoffs

"I am concerned about the economy. I was the first person laid off."

> —Al Gore (vice president, 1993–2001), in a 2001 speech to biotech executives in California

★ Leadership

"He held the leader's coat. He was a great assistant . . . not a leader."

> —Andrew Cuomo (2002 New York gubernatorial candidate), arguing that New York Governor George Pataki's leadership during the September 11 crisis was dwarfed by Rudy Giuliani's leadership

★ Legacy

"If the American people don't love me, their descendants will."

> —Lyndon Johnson (president, 1963–1969)

★ Legislation

"This is the most important bill of the session. . . . I have not read the bill."

> —Sherman Copelin (Louisiana state representative, 1984–2000), on a bill to prevent flooding

"Don't worry. If this bill was too complicated, they wouldn't have let me handle it."

> —Troy Hebert (Louisiana state representative, 1995–)

"As many of you know, I'm a former coroner, and I declare Mr. Riddle's bill dead!"

>—Jack Smith (Louisiana state representative, 1991–)

⭐ Lengthy Speeches

"It wasn't my finest hour. It wasn't even my finest half-hour."

>—Bill Clinton (president, 1993–2001), on his protracted speech nominating Michael Dukakis at the 1988 Democratic National Convention

⭐ Lobbying

"To call him a prostitute would elevate him."

>—Oscar Goodman (mayor of Las Vegas, 1999–), on John Sununu, chief of staff in the first Bush administration, who lobbied to allow nuclear waste storage at Nevada's Yucca Mountain

"If you don't like the president, it costs you ninety bucks to fly to Washington to picket. If you don't like the governor, it costs you sixty bucks to fly to Albany to picket. If you don't like me, ninety cents."

>—Ed Koch (mayor of New York, 1978–1989)

🐴 Lockboxes

"My plan to put Social Security in an ironclad lock-box has gotten a lot of attention recently, and I'm glad about that. But I'm afraid that it's overshadowing some vitally important proposals. For instance, I'll put Medicaid in a walk-in closet. I'll put the Community Reinvestment Act in a secured gym locker. I'll put NASA funding in a hermetically sealed Ziploc bag."

> —Al Gore (2000 presidential nominee),
> joking at the Al Smith dinner in 2000

🐴 Loopholes

"There are more loopholes in the U.S. Tax Code than those old hockey nets at the Boston Garden. Beam me up. The truth is, America keeps shipping jobs and money overseas, and America is getting in return two truckloads of mangoes and two baseball players to be named later."

> —James Traficant (representative from
> Ohio, 1985–2002)

🐴 Lying

"I tried to walk a fine line between acting lawfully and testifying falsely, but I now recognize that I did not fully accomplish that goal."

> —Bill Clinton (president 1993–2001), on lying to the grand jury about Monica Lewinsky

"Rather than lie to the grand jury itself, the president lied about his relationship with Ms. Lewinsky to senior aides, and those aides then conveyed the false story to the grand jury."

> —Bruce Lindsey (senior assistant to President Clinton)

"If a president of the United States ever lied to the American people, he should resign."

> —Bill Clinton, commenting on President Nixon and the Watergate scandal while running for Congress in 1974

🐴 Management Style

"When things haven't gone well for you, call in a secretary or a staff man and chew him out. You will sleep better and they will appreciate the attention."

—Lyndon Johnson (president, 1963–1969)

🐴 Marriage

"I don't see any difference between interracial marriages and same-sex marriages."

—Carol Moseley Braun (2004 presidential candidate)

"We must not be in a relationship with a Democratic Party that takes us for granted. We must no longer be the political mistress of the Democratic Party. A mistress is where they take you out to have fun, but then can't take you home to Mama and Daddy. Either we're going to get married in 2004 or we're going to find some folks who ain't ashamed to be seen with us."

—Al Sharpton (2004 presidential candidate)

⋆ Mass Transportation

"Mine is a form of municipal transportation, although it is exclusive to me."

> —Willie Brown (mayor of San Francisco, 1996–2004). Brown traveled to the San Francisco Giants' opening game in his official Lincoln Town Car. Mass transit officials had encouraged use of public transportation to the park.

⋆ Me

"Would you mind mentioning my name?"

> —Joe Lieberman (2004 presidential candidate), to President George W. Bush, upon hearing that Bush was headed to electorally important Iowa

"I'm a powerful SOB, you know that?"

> —Lyndon Johnson

"See how liberal I'm becoming!"

> —Hillary Rodham Clinton, writing to a friend while a student at Wellesley College

"I am Al Gore, and I used to be the next president of the United States of America."

> —Al Gore

"Vice president of the government in exile."

> —Joe Lieberman (2000 vice-presidential candidate)

"The New Jersey Wen Ho Lee."

> —Robert Torricelli (senator from New Jersey, 1997–2002), after federal prosecutors dropped charges accusing him of receiving illegal campaign funds from David Chang (who gave him an $8,100 Rolex watch, Italian suits, and a large-screen TV). Wen Ho Lee was held in solitary confinement for alleged improper handling of nuclear secrets.

"No, it's not a joke. I really am Al Gore. How can I prove it to you? . . . No, it's me, Al Gore. . . . Mary, it's Vice President Al Gore. . . . No, it's *not* Michael."

> —Al Gore, making a get-out-the-vote phone call at his Manchester, New Hampshire, campaign headquarters in 2000

"Great things happen in small places. Jesus was born in Bethlehem. Jesse Jackson was born in Greenville."

> —Jesse Jackson (1988 presidential candidate), during the 1988 presidential campaign

Media

"Many of them are so dumb they could throw themselves at the ground and miss."

> —James Traficant (representative from Ohio, 1985–2002)

Melting Pots

"I hear that melting-pot stuff a lot, and all I can say is we haven't melted."

> —Jesse Jackson (1988 presidential candidate)

Meta-Narrative

"The meta-narrative is that Gore is stiff, Bush mangles his words."

> —Al Gore, speaking to his class at Columbia University in 2001

🐴 Howard Metzenbaum

"The senator from B'nai B'rith."

> —Ernest Hollings (senator from South
> Carolina, 1965–2004), on then–Ohio
> Democratic Senator Howard Metzenbaum,
> a strong supporter of Israel, during a
> Senate debate on voluntary prayer in
> schools. Hollings later apologized.

🐴 Military

"We won't always have the strongest military."

> —Howard Dean (2004 presidential
> candidate)

🐴 Misdeeds

"Was I ever arrested? No. But I'm not going to cata-
log my misdeeds, of which there were a significant
number."

> —Howard Dean

🐴 Missing Persons Bureau

"Bush said after September 11, we've got to go after
bin Laden. Yet he can't bin Laden . . . He can't find

the weapons. Now we've got to take pride that Saddam Hussein is still alive; we can't find him. I promise you if I'm elected, President Bush will not be in charge of the missing persons bureau."

—Al Sharpton (2004 presidential candidate)

Moderation

"I have finally figured out what the Republican orators mean by what they call 'moderate progressivism.' All they mean is: 'Don't just do something, stand there.'"

—Adlai Stevenson (1952 and 1956 presidential candidate)

Monica

"Maybe there will be a simple, innocent explanation. I don't think so, because I think we would have offered that up already."

—Mike McCurry (press secretary to President Clinton)

"I have learned over the last many years being involved in politics, and especially since my husband first started running for president, that the best thing to do in these cases is just to be patient, take a deep breath, and the truth will come out."

> —Hillary Rodham Clinton (first lady, 1993–2001), on the *Today* show, January, 27, 1998

"If all that were proven true, I think that would be a very serious offense. This is not going to be proven true."

> —Hillary Rodham Clinton, on the *Today* show, January 27, 1998

"Gulping for air, I started crying and yelling at him, 'What do you mean? What are you saying? Why did you lie to me?'"

> —Hillary Rodham Clinton, recounting her reaction when her husband told her about Monica Lewinsky

"I will never understand what was going through my husband's mind that day. All I know is that Bill told his staff and our friends the same story he told me: that nothing improper went on. Why he felt the need to deceive me and others is his own story, and he needs to tell it in his own way."

> —Hillary Rodham Clinton, in her book, *Living History*

"I think he [Bill Clinton] should have made it very clear to Monica, to her family, all those forces need to feel that there's no fall guy. The responsibility should have been in his lap."

> —Jesse Jackson (1988 presidential candidate)

"I was never a bad person. I made some mistakes, but I just needed to mature. I'm doing that."

> —Monica Lewinsky (Clinton White House intern)

"You were always there when she was around, right? We were never really alone. You could see and hear everything. Monica came on to me, and I never touched her, right?"

> —Bill Clinton, coaching Betty Currie, his personal secretary, on her grand jury testimony

"You stupid, stupid, stupid bastard. My God, Bill: how could you risk everything for that?"

—Hillary Rodham Clinton

"I'm really sorry for everything that's happened. And I hate Linda Trip."

—Monica Lewinsky

Motherhood

"There must be something in the home cooking Barbara was whipping up."

—Terry McAuliffe (chairman, Democratic National Committee), accusing both President Bush and Florida Governor Jeb Bush of budget mismanagement and broken promises

Multitasking

"I have a brain and a uterus, and I use both."

—Patricia Schroeder (representative from Colorado, 1973–1996), asked "How can you be both a lawmaker and a mother?"

 Rupert Murdock

"You scare the hell out of me."

> —Maxine Waters (representative from California, 1991–), to media mogul Rupert Murdock when he sought a House committee's permission to buy Direct TV

Narcissism

"While Bill talked about social change, I embodied it."

> —Hillary Rodham Clinton (first lady, 1993–2001), in her book, *Living History*

NASA

"Now NASA is on an unmanned space mission to the moon. I think NASA should redirect and have an unmanned space mission to Washington, D.C., and try to find out if there is any intelligent life left in the nation's capital."

> —James Traficant (representative from Ohio, 1985–2002)

🫏 New Money

"My definition of new money is money that's in my pocket today that was in somebody else's pocket yesterday."

> —Jerry Luke LeBlanc (Louisiana state representative, 1989–)

🫏 Richard Nixon

"Nixon is the kind of politician who would cut down a redwood tree, then mount the stump for a conservation speech."

> —Adlai Stevenson (1952 and 1956 presidential nominee)

"He's one of the few people in the history of the country to run for high office talking out of both sides of his mouth at the same time and lying out of both sides."

> —Harry Truman (president, 1945–1953)

🫏 Nobody

"I've been here a long time, and I don't trust anybody. And when I say anybody, I mean nobody."

> —John Travis (Louisiana state representative, 1996–2000)

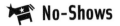 No-Shows

"Your political capital is the equivalent of Confederate dollars."

> —Kwesi Mfume (NAACP executive director, and former Democratic congressman), on George W. Bush and three Democratic presidential candidates who did not show up for the group's annual convention

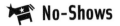 Notoriety

"There are pluses and minuses. The plus is that I'm known by everybody. The minus is that I'm known by everybody."

> —Jerry Springer (abortive candidate for the U.S. Senate from Ohio in 2004)

"I don't know if you've been following the polls. But I think it will actually be news to most people that I'm running for president of the United States."

> —John Edwards (2004 presidential candidate), announcing his candidacy on *The Daily Show* on Comedy Central

🐴 Opposing Counsel

"I want you to disregard all the opposing counsel has said. . . . I think they should be handcuffed, chained to a fence, and flogged. . . . And if they lie again, I'm going to go over there and kick them in the crotch."

—James Traficant

🐴 Opponents

"One-fifth of the people are against everything all the time."

—Robert Kennedy (1968 presidential candidate)

🐴 Organizational Charts

"You don't kill terrorists by moving boxes on an organizational chart."

—David Obey (representative from Wisconsin, 1969–), on the Department of Homeland Security

"The question is whether shifting the deck chairs on the *Titanic* is the way to go."

—Ted Kennedy (senator from Massachusetts, 1963–), on the Department of Homeland Security

🫏 Osama bin Laden

"One could say that Osama bin Laden and these non-nation-state fighters with religious purposes are very similar to those kind of atypical revolutionaries that helped to cut off the British crown."

> —Marcy Kaptur (representative from Ohio, 1983–), comparing Osama bin Laden to the Founding Fathers. She later apologized for the statement.

"He's been out in these countries for decades building roads, building schools, building infrastructure, building day-care facilities, building health-care facilities, and the people are extremely grateful. It made their lives better."

> —Patty Murray (senator from Washington, 1993–), speaking to a high school honors class. Two days later, she issued a statement that "Osama bin Laden is an evil terrorist."

"This guy has more videos than a rock star."

> —Al Sharpton (2004 presidential candidate)

🐴 Paralysis

"I've seen many politicians paralyzed in the legs as myself, but I've seen more of them who were paralyzed in the head."

> —George Wallace (four-time governor of Alabama)

🐴 Pardons

"I knew nothing about my brother's involvement in these pardons. . . . I had no knowledge whatsoever."

> —Hillary Rodham Clinton (first lady, 1993–2001), on the fact that her brother, Hugh Rodham, made $400,000 in legal fees securing presidential pardons for his clients

🐴 Patriotism

"If the economy continues in the tank, then I think it is obviously a very, very positive thing for the Democrats."

> —Gerald McEntee (president of the American Federation of State, County, and Municipal Employees)

🐴 Patronizing

"Maybe, at times, I was a little wooden and stiff, and I sighed too much and people said I was too patronizing. Patronizing, of course, means talking to people like they're stupid."

> —Al Gore, joking during the monologue on *Saturday Night Live* on December 14, 2002

"If you give the impression you're a smarty pants, that's not good, for sure."

> —Al Gore, during the 2000 presidential campagin

🐴 Peace

"I've been working on the idea of creating a Department of Peace, where nonviolence would become an organizing principle in our society, not only for international problems, but for domestic, as well. . . . What I envision is nothing less than a transformation of the social and political structure through changing the consciousness of the nation and the world about matters of war and peace; to see peace and not war as being inevitable; and to see a way in which the human experience can evolve and unfold in higher expressions, instead of getting caught in a downward spiral."

>—Dennis Kucinich (2004 Democratic presidential candidate)

Political Consultants

"I not only felt they believed in me, but I felt they hated my opponent."

>—John Norquist (mayor of Milwaukee, 1988–2004), explaining why he liked his media consultants, Karl Struble and David Eichenbaum

Political Philosophy

"I'm a liberal, conservative, radical, middle-of-the-road centrist Democrat."

>—Richard Dreyfuss (actor and Democratic activist)

Politicians

"A politician is a person who approaches every subject with an open mouth."

>—Adlai Stevenson (1952 and 1956 Democratic presidential nominee)

Politics

"Being in politics is like being a football coach. You have to be smart enough to understand the game, and dumb enough to think it's important."

> —Eugene McCarthy (senator from Minnesota, 1959–1970)

Pork Barreling

"You can't have a Christmas tree during Lent."

> —Barney Frank (representative from Massachusetts, 1981–), on pork-barrel spending added to a military benefits bill

Post-Presidential Plans

"I have to work. It costs a lot of money to support a senator."

> —Bill Clinton, just prior to leaving the presidency

Predators

"The other thing we have to do is to take seriously the role in this problem of . . . older men who prey on underage women. . . . There are consequences to decisions and . . . one way or other, people always end up being held accountable."

> —Bill Clinton, in a 1996 speech endorsing a national effort against teen pregnancy

Presidency

"Move over. This is your president."

> —Lyndon Johnson (president, 1963–1969), to a White House secretary who woke up at Johnson's Texas ranch to find LBJ climbing into bed with her

"I'm having a great time being presi—being a senator from New York."

> —Hillary Rodham Clinton, asked at the National Press Club whether she intended to run for the presidency

"I once told Nixon that the presidency is like being a jackass in a hailstorm. There's nothing to do but stand there and take it."

> —Lyndon Johnson

"The best reason I can think of for not running for president of the United States is that you have to shave twice a day."

> —Adlai Stevenson (1952 and 1956 Democratic presidential nominee)

"All the president is is a glorified public relations man who spends his time flattering, kissing, and kicking people to get them to do what they are supposed to do anyway."

> —Harry Truman (president, 1945–1953)

"When I'm president, we'll have executive orders to overcome any wrong thing the Supreme Court does tomorrow or any other day."

> —Dick Gephardt (2004 presidential candidate), apparently unaware that the president has no authority to issue executive orders to overcome Supreme Court decisions

"Frankly, I don't mind not being president. I just mind that someone else is."

> —Ted Kennedy (senator from Massachusetts, 1963–), joking at the Gridiron Club in 1986

⭐ Priorities

"Webb, I want to know two things: who killed JFK, and are there UFOs?"

> —Bill Clinton, to Assistant Attorney General Webster Hubbell, in 1993

⭐ Prison

"It's like going to a very inexpensive spa."

> —Buddy Cianci (former mayor of Providence, Rhode Island), on reporting to a federal prison to serve a five-year sentence for bribery

⭐ Privacy

"I believe in a zone of privacy."

> —Hillary Rodham Clinton (first lady, 1993–2001), at a press conference while promoting her book, *Living History*

⭐ Procedures

"[There is] no procedural agreement on the procedures."

> —Bob Kerrey (senator from Nebraska, 1989–2000)

⭐ Pronunciation

"You shouldn't be governor unless you can pronounce the name of the state."

> —Gray Davis (governor of California,
> 1999–2003), during the 2003 California
> recall campaign, referring to Arnold
> Schwarzenegger's "Kah-lee-fohr-nyah"
> pronunciation. In response, Schwarzeneg-
> ger said, "He doesn't like the way I say the
> word California, because I say Cal-ee-for-
> nia rather than Cal-a-fornia. But there's
> many other words that he doesn't like.
> *Lost jobs*, he doesn't like that word. He
> doesn't like *blackout*. He doesn't like
> *energy crisis*. And he definitely doesn't like
> *recall*." Three days later, Davis said, "It
> was a poor joke. I shouldn't have done it."

⭐ Public Approval Ratings

"If they reach 60 percent, then he can start dating
again."

> —Ernest Hollings (senator from South
> Carolina, 1965–2004), on President
> Clinton's approval ratings in public
> opinion polls

🐴 Qualifications

"I can put two sentences together, and I know I can pronounce the word *nuclear*."

> —Dick Gephardt (2004 presidential candidate), on his prospects in a debate with President Bush

"In America, anybody may become president, and I suppose it's just one of the risks you take."

> —Adlai Stevenson (1952 and 1956 presidential nominee)

"I am working for the time when unqualified blacks, browns, and women join the unqualified men in running the government."

> —Sissy Farenthold (Texas state representative, 1969–1972)

"Anyone can be elected governor. I'm proof of that."

> —Joe Frank Harris (governor of Georgia, 1983–1991)

"I will not deny that there are men in the district better qualified than I to go to Congress, but gentlemen, these men are not in the race."

—Sam Rayburn (representative from Texas, 1913–1962)

Race

"I'm the only white politician that ever talks about race in front of white audiences."

—Howard Dean (2004 presidential candidate)

Rainbow Coalition

"Blackbow."

—Ernest Hollings (senator from South Carolina, 1965–2004), on Jesse Jackson's Rainbow Coalition

🫏 Rape

"The truth of the matter is, I have been publicly raped."

> —Robert Torricelli (senator from New Jersey, 1997–2002), on investigations of his finances

🫏 Ronald Reagan

"I was cooking breakfast this morning for my kids, and I thought, 'He's just like a Teflon frying pan. Nothing sticks to him.'"

> —Patricia Schroeder (representative from Colorado, 1973–1996), in April 1983. Reagan came to be known as "the Teflon president."

"You've got to be careful quoting Ronald Reagan, because when you quote him accurately, it's called mudslinging."

> —Walter Mondale (1984 presidential nominee)

🐴 Recessions

"I was governor for so long that I got to serve through not one but two Bush recessions."

> —Howard Dean (2004 presidential candidate). Dean was governor of Vermont from 1991 to 2003.

🐴 Recollections

"Since I was a little boy, I've heard about the Iowa caucuses."

> —Bill Clinton, during the 1996 presidential campaign. The Iowa caucuses began in 1972, when Clinton was a Rhodes Scholar at Oxford University.

🐴 Records

"Sometimes we jest up here. Sometimes we say things that we would not want to be recorded."

> —Ron Landry (Louisiana state senator, 1976–2000), opposing a resolution to record Senate debates

🐴 Recovery

"Nothing beats C–SPAN on drugs."

> —John Kerry (2004 presidential candidate),
> joking about his recovery from prostate
> surgery

🐴 Regime Change

"What we need now is not just a regime change in
Saddam Hussein and Iraq, but we need a regime
change in the United States."

> —John Kerry, in a New Hampshire speech

🐴 Regrets

"I often get asked the question: 'Is there anything I
would have done differently?' I say, 'Yeah, there is.
If I had to do it over again, I would have kissed
Tipper longer.'"

> —Al Gore (2000 presidential nominee), in
> 2001

🐴 Religious Schools

"Thanks to the U.S. Supreme Court, you'll be able
to use public money to send your kids to General
Beauregard Bigot Private Academy, Fundamental-

ist Football, and Frequent Drug Tests. They have these religious schools that teach these kids insanity like the earth is five thousand years old, where the Pope is a demon. I don't want my tax dollars going to that kind of crap. You can practice religion until you fall out. I don't want to pay for somebody else's bigotry."

> —James Carville (political consultant)

🐴 Republicans

"I promise just to serve two terms. Republicans do it differently. They just have the son repeat the father's whole first term."

> —John Kerry (2004 presidential candidate)

"I have to confess that it's crossed my mind that you could not be a Republican and a Christian."

> —Hillary Rodham Clinton (senator from New York, 2001–)

"Did you get this shit out?"

> —Al Gore, to White House speechwriters in April 1995, insisting that they remove excessive praise for Republicans

"I have been thinking that I would make a proposition to my Republican friends. . . . That if they will stop telling lies about the Democrats, we will stop telling the truth about them."

> —Adlai Stevenson (1952 and 1956 presidential nominee)

"The Democratic Party at its worst is better than the Republican Party at its best."

> —Lyndon Johnson (president, 1963–1969)

"The trouble with the Republican Party is that it has not had a new idea in thirty years. I am not speaking as a politician; I am speaking as an historian."

> —Woodrow Wilson (president, 1913–1921)

"Suppose you were an idiot. And suppose you were a Republican. But I repeat myself."

> —Harry Truman (president, 1945–1953)

"Republicans bring out Colin Powell and J. C. Watts because they have no program, no policy. They have no love and no joy. They'd rather take pictures with black children than feed them."

> —Donna Brazile (manager, Gore 2000 presidential campaign)

"If you don't think it's a gamble to put a man in the White House who believes we should have guns in church, who thinks the Taliban is a rock band, who was such a failure as a businessman that his company was nicknamed 'El-Busto,' who wants to turn our Social Security system into a Wall Street boiler room, who can't name a single thing he disagrees with Jerry Falwell and Pat Robertson on, who smeared a bona fide hero named John McCain, and whose principal policy proposal is to give America's surplus to the idle rich in the form of a $1.3 trillion tax cut, you're either nuts or a Republican."

— Paul Begala (Clinton White House staffer)

🫏 Respect

"The tribes, I believe, are showing the same respect I showed them when they had nothing. I think they're showing their friendship by helping me in trying to basically level the playing field."

> —Cruz Bustamante (California gubernatorial candidate, 2003), on his acceptance of $2 million in campaign contributions from Indian casinos

🐴 Retirement

"It's time I go out and work and make a living."

> —Ernest Hollings (senator from South Carolina, 1965–2004), retiring from the U.S. Senate after almost forty years, at age eighty-one

🐴 Rights

"Every man has a right to a Saturday night bath."

> —Lyndon Johnson

🐴 Right Wingers

"For those of you scoring at home, the Clintons have been cleared on Whitewater, cleared on the travel office, cleared on the file matter, cleared on the vandalism, cleared on Madison Guaranty, cleared on Vince Foster's suicide. The right wing is zero-for-life going after the Clintons. They ought to get a life."

> —Paul Begala (Clinton White House staffer)

 Rival Supporters

"A bunch of wetbacks."

> —Ernest Hollings (senator from South Carolina, 1965–2004) referring to supporters of California Senator Alan Cranston, a rival for the 1984 Democratic presidential nomination

 Rocket Science

"This isn't rocket science here."

> —Tom Daschle (senator from South Dakota, 1987–), denouncing spending billions on President Bush's proposed space-based defense system

Donald Rumsfeld

"If I were still secretary of state listening to the current secretary of defense, I'd be tempted to press the mute button."

> —Madeleine Albright (secretary of state, 1997–2001)

🐴 Running Mates

"Lieberman-Buchanan: a ticket only a mother could love. Lieberman-Buchanan: building a bridge to the fourteenth century."

> —Joe Lieberman (2004 presidential candidate), joking about the idea of Pat Buchanan as his running mate

🐴 Ruthlessness

"Now I can go back to being ruthless."

> —Robert Kennedy (senator from New York, 1965–1968), joking after winning his 1964 election to the U.S. Senate

🐴 Saddam's Sons

"Are you going to sleep any safer tonight knowing that these two bums are dead?"

> —Charles Rangel (representative from New York, 1971–), on the death of Uday and Qusay Hussein

🐴 Safe Money

"The Republicans have gone from safe sex to safe money. I predict that the Republican concept of safe money will require millionaires to use condoms on all their safe money and their credit cards."

> —James Traficant (representative from Ohio, 1985–2002)

🐴 Schlemiels

"Our struggle today is not to have a female Einstein appointed as an assistant professor. It is for a woman schlemiel to get as quickly promoted as a male schlemiel."

> —Bella Abzug (representative from New York, 1971–1976)

🐴 Secrecy

"Your budget by now is about as big a secret as my sexuality."

> —Barney Frank (representative from Massachusetts, 1981–), speaking at a CIA gay pride celebration, on his efforts to publicize federal spending on intelligence

⭐ Secretary of the Treasury

"You are no Alexander Hamilton."

> —Robert Byrd (senator from West Virginia, 1959–), to then–Secretary of the Treasury Paul O'Neill

⭐ Self-Perception

"I think I am the first black president."

> —Bill Clinton, repeating the designation first bestowed by Toni Morrison

"I'm not a slasher and burner. Everyone thinks my team is, but I'm a nice guy."

> —Gray Davis (governor of California, 1999–2003).

"I could be an incredible voice in the Senate. Why? Because the media will cover me every single day."

> —Jerry Springer (abortive candidate for the U.S. Senate from Ohio in 2004)

"Both in theory and practice, I could have been the strongest candidate."

> —Gary Hart (abortive 2004 presidential candidate)

"I was a frat boy and the girls hated me."

—Bill Clinton

September 11

"The roads in Missouri were much more terrifying to me than the attacks on the World Trade Center, because I really did think my life was far more at risk."

—Kathleen Sebelius (governor of Kansas, 2003–), during the 2002 campaign

Sex

"Sex is a bad thing because it rumples the clothes."

—Jaqueline Kennedy Onassis (first lady, 1961–1963)

Sexual Harassment

"I would never approach a small-breasted woman."

—Bill Clinton (president, 1993–2001), denying that he had sexually harassed Kathleen Willey

"You're smart. Let's keep this to ourselves."

—Bill Clinton, to Paula Jones

🐴 Sexual Indiscretions

"I figure we got 532 to go."

> —James Moran (representative from Virginia, 1991–), after three congressmen admitted sexual indiscretions

🐴 Showing Up

"Woody Allen wasn't talking about foreign policy when he said that 85 percent of life is just showing up."

> —Tom Daschle (senator from South Dakota, 1987–), criticizing Bush administration foreign policy officials for not actively participating in international meetings

🐴 Sighs

"I put all my sighs in a lock box."

> —Al Gore (2000 presidential nominee), after his second presidential debate in 2000 with George W. Bush

🐴 Signatures

"I don't sign skin."

> —Al Gore, to a young voter during the 2000 presidential campaign

🐴 Sincerity

"Always be sincere, even if you don't mean it."

—Harry Truman (president, 1945–1953)

🐴 Sleeping Plans

"I'm going to spend the night with a public school teacher in Michigan tonight."

—Al Gore, at a campaign 2000 rally in Cincinnati

🐴 Smarts

"It took him an hour and a half to watch *60 Minutes.*"

—Edwin Edwards (four-term governor of Louisiana), on David Treen, his opponent in the 1983 Louisiana gubernatorial race

"You think you are so smart. I'll tell you how smart I am. I went all the way through USL [the University of Southwestern Louisiana] and I have never read a book all the way through."

—Paul Hardy (1991 Louisiana gubernatorial candidate)

🐴 Smoke-Filled Rooms

"You say the training takes place in smoke-filled rooms full of confusion. Wouldn't it be cheaper just to train them in the Senate?"

> —Jack Smith (Louisiana state representative, 1991–), during committee debate on firefighter training legislation

🐴 Smut

"Politics is my hobby. Smut is my profession."

> —Larry Flynt (publisher of *Hustler* and 2003 California gubernatorial candidate)

🐴 Social Class

"There are a lot of people who have yachts and sail in Martha's Vineyard. Other people play tennis and belong to River Club or Burning Tree. My poor textile worker, when he gets off in the afternoooon, the best thing he can do is go up on the front porch, sit in the rocker, and put his feet up on the rail, and light up a Lucky and relax."

> —Ernest Hollings (senator from South Carolina, 1965–2004)

🫏 Sombreros

"Do you own sombreros? Do you know the Mexican hat dance?"

> —Sidney Yates (representative from Illinois, 1949–1998), to a group of Hispanic high school students

🫏 Some of My Best Friends

"I have in some ways a special relationship with the African-American community because of my college career. I had two African-American roommates in college."

> —Howard Dean (2004 presidential candidate)

🫏 Speaking Abilities

"Some people think I faked it for eight years before 100 million people."

> —Bill Clinton (president, 1993–2001), on his speaking abilities

🫏 Stardust

"The enemy of the stars becomes us. We become the energy of the stars. Stardust and spirit unite and we begin: one with the universe, whole and holy. From one source, endless creative energy, bursting forth, kinetic elemental; we, the earth, water, and fire-source of nearly fifteen billion years of cosmic spiraling."

> —Dennis Kucinich (2004 presidential
> candidate), in the *Journal of Conscious
> Evolution*

Starr Report

"It's not clear what the purpose of the report is other than to promote Robert Ray's Senate campaign, Monica Lewinsky's HBO special, and the Paula Jones vs. Tonya Harding boxing match."

> —Jennifer Palmieri (Clinton White House
> spokesperson), on the Starr Report on the
> Monica Lewinsky scandal

State Legislature

"We're in the hands of the state legislature and God, but at the moment, the state legislature has more to say than God."

> —Ed Koch (mayor of New York, 1978–1989),
> asking for additional aid to New York City
> in 1986

⭐ Statistics

"Statistics are like bathing suits. What they expose is interesting, but what they cover is vital."

> —Raymond Jetson (Louisiana state
> representative, 1984–1999)

⭐ Straight Talk Express

"I really don't like the idea of a federal balanced-budget amendment, but I am very tempted. . . . You might just have to do it. I hate to do it because we didn't have to do it in Vermont."

> —Howard Dean (2004 presidential
> candidate)

⭐ Strategy

"It's our new secret debate strategy for undecided voters: Vote for the candidate with the best hair."

> —Kelly Benander (spokesman, John Kerry
> for President campaign)

 Substance

"When I hear your new ideas, I'm reminded of that ad, 'Where's the beef?'"

> —Walter Mondale (vice president, 1977–1981), during a March 11, 1984, Democratic presidential candidates debate, to Gary Hart

Substance SUVs

"The pickup owners of this nation might get screwed in all this gas-guzzling talk about SUVs and vans."

> —Zell Miller (senator from Georgia, 1999–2004)

"I hear some news from Washington
Of a crackpot scheme to raise some mon
It's an unkind way to raise a buck
And it adds more cost to my pickup truck."

> —Zell Miller, coauthor of "The Talking Pickup Truck Blues"

"Sure, an SUV is classy travel
But it ain't much good for haulin' gravel
Or hay or seed or bovine feces
So please, don't make my pickup truck an
   endangered species."

> —Zell Miller, the second verse of "The
> Talking Pickup Truck Blues"

🐴 Tardiness

"I was on other media broadcasts trying to demean you and everybody else."

> —James Traficant (representative from
> Ohio, 1985–2002), explaining why he was
> late for a media interview

🐴 Taxes

"I don't need Bush's tax cut. I have never worked a [bleeping] day in my life."

> —Patrick Kennedy (representative from
> Rhode Island, 1995–)

"It's not 'spic' or 'nigger' anymore. They say, 'Let's cut taxes.'"

> —Charles Rangel (representative from New York, 1971–)

"It was like Jim Jones giving out Kool Aid. It tastes good, but it will kill you."

> —Al Sharpton (2004 presidential candidate), on George W. Bush's tax cuts

"There's a huge overpayment in taxes. It's like the Elvis Presley song, 'Return to Sender.'"

> —Zell Miller, on his support for George W. Bush's tax cut

"[Republicans] would rather shoot their mothers than raise taxes."

> —Gray Davis (governor of California, 1999–2003), during the 2003 recall election

"This plan is obscene!"

> —Tom Daschle (senator from South Dakota, 1987–), on President George W. Bush's tax cut

"I'll tell you the whole story about the budget. Probably there are people in this room still mad at me at that budget because you think I raised your taxes too much. It might surprise you to know I think I raised them too much, too."

—Bill Clinton (president, 1993–2001), on October 18, 1995

"Tax reform means 'Don't tax me, don't tax me, tax that fellow behind the tree.'"

—Russell Long (senator from Louisiana, 1947–1986)

⭐ Tell–All Books

"I calculated that for every dollar I made on a book, I'd have to spend two dollars on therapy for just reliving it, so I'm not writing a book."

—Joe Lockhart (press secretary to President Clinton)

⭐ Term Limitation

"You'd have to throw me out."

—Bill Clinton, on what he would do if the 22nd Amendment didn't limit presidents to two terms

🫏 Textiles

"I bought it at the same place where you got that wig, Sam."

> —Ernest Hollings (senator from South
> Carolina, 1965–2004), to Sam Donaldson,
> on *This Week with David Brinkley*.
> Donaldson had said, "Senator, you're from
> the great textile-producing state of South
> Carolina. Is it true you have a Korean
> tailor?"

🫏 These People

"These people are just like us. They love their children and keep themselves clean."

> —Paul Hardy (1991 Louisiana gubernatorial
> candidate), after spending a night at the
> Desire Housing project in New Orleans

🫏 Things

"Things happen more frequently in the future than they do in the past."

> —Booth Gardner (governor of Washington,
> 1985–1993)

🐴 Clarence Thomas

"Clarence Thomas is my color, but he's not my kind."

> —Al Sharpton (2004 presidential candidate)

🐴 Strom Thurmond

"I think this is his last laugh."

> —Joe Biden (senator from Rhode Island, 1973–), on being selected by Strom Thurmond to deliver a eulogy

"[It's] sad because the poor fellow doesn't have any place to go, if you think on it. He doesn't have a home and someone has said the best nursing home is the U.S. Senate. He's got a car, a place to stay, and somebody over there at night at the apartment with him. He's well enough; he's in the pool for a few laps."

> —Ernest Hollings (senator from South Carolina, 1965–2004), on why his Senate colleague Strom Thurmond (then ninety-eight) did not retire

🐴 Time Management

"You better call my dad. My mom's pretty busy."

> —Chelsea Clinton (daughter of Bill and Hillary Clinton), to her school nurse

⭐ Today and Tomorrow

"Today the real problem is the future."

> —Richard J. Daley (mayor of Chicago,
> 1955–1976)

"We're the party of Tomorrowland. They're the party of Fantasyland. We're the party of Main Street USA. They're the party of the Pirates of Enron."

> —Al Gore (2000 presidential candidate), in
> April 2002 at the Florida Democratic Party
> convention

⭐ John Tower

"Put in Mr. Alcoholic Abuser as secretary of defense? Man, what are you talking about in this body?"

> —Ernest Hollings (senator from South
> Carolina, 1965–2004), on the 1989
> nomination of Texas Senator John Tower to
> be secretary of defense

⭐ Travel

"I've traveled more this year than any other living human being, and if I traveled any more I wouldn't be living."

> —Walter Mondale (vice president, 1977–1981)

★ Trickle-Down Economics

"I believe every worker in America is tired of being trickled on by George W. Bush."

> —John Kerry (2004 presidential candidate)

★ Truthfulness

"What a liar!"

> —Daniel Inouye (senator from Hawaii, 1963–), into an open mike while John Ehrlichman (a Nixon White House adviser) testified during the Watergate hearings

★ Twinkies

"They fry it in soy oil. We actually checked that out ahead of time. Because I just knew some sonofabitch would want to know."

> —Joe Lieberman (2004 presidential candidate), explaining that he knew that the deep-fried Twinkie he was eating at the Iowa State Fair was kosher

★ Two-Party System

"The two-party system has given this country the war of Lyndon Johnson, the Watergate of Nixon, and the incompetence of Carter. Saying we should keep the

two-party system simply because it is working is
like saying the *Titanic* voyage was a success
because a few people survived on life-rafts."

> —Eugene McCarthy (senator from
> Minnesota, 1959–1970)

🐴 Ulcers

"I'm not the type to get ulcers. I give them."

> —Ed Koch (mayor of New York City,
> 1978–1989)

🐴 Understanding

"So people with nothing between their ears, like
you, can understand what I'm talking about!"

> —Edwin Edwards (four-time governor of
> Louisiana), asked during a 1983 debate
> by opponent David Treen, "Why do you
> keep talking out of both sides of your
> mouth?"

![] Unemployment

"When we're unemployed, we're called lazy; when the whites are unemployed, it's called a depression."

> —Jesse Jackson (1988 presidential candidate)

![] University

"The use of a university is to make young gentle-men as unlike their fathers as possible."

> —Woodrow Wilson (president, 1913–1921)

![] Vast Right Wing Conspiracy

"That'll teach them to —— with us."

> —Hillary Rodham Clinton (first lady, 1993–2001), to aides, after appearing on the *Today* show on January 27, 1998, to discuss "the vast right-wing conspiracy"

🐴 Jesse Ventura

"I'm even thinking about a feather boa."

> —Al Gore, during the 2000 presidential
> campaign, on his friendship with Jesse
> Ventura

🐴 Vermont

"It's sure nice being welcomed back to Vermont
being a liberal pinko."

> —Howard Dean (2004 presidential
> candidate)

🐴 Vice Presidency

"You better take advantage of the good cigars. You
don't get much else in that job."

> —Tip O'Neill (representative from
> Massachusetts, 1953–1986), to then–Vice
> President Walter Mondale

🐴 Victory

"I know I can beat George Bush. Why? Because Al
Gore and I already did."

> —Joe Lieberman (2004 presidential
> candidate)

🫏 Vision

"My vision is to make the most diverse state on earth, and we have people from every planet on the earth in this state, of people from every planet, of every country on earth."

>—Gray Davis (governor of California, 1999–2003)

🫏 Voodoo Economics

"I'd call it a new version of voodoo economics, but I'm afraid that would give witch doctors a bad name."

>—Geraldine Ferraro (1984 vice presidential nominee), on the Republican Party platform

🫏 Voters

"The biggest danger is for a politician to shake hands with a man who is physically stronger, has been drinking, and is voting for the other guy."

>—William Proxmire (senator from Wisconsin, 1957–1988), in 1966

"I'd win in a landslide if weird people voted."

—Jerry Springer (abortive candidate for the
U.S. Senate from Ohio in 2004)

🐴 War Hero

"It's easy: they sank my boat."

—John Kennedy (president, 1961–1963),
asked how he became a war hero

🐴 Washington

"I remember when I first came to Washington. For
the first six months you wonder how the hell you
ever got there. For the next six months you wonder
how the hell the rest of them got there."

—Harry Truman (president, 1945–1953)

"My father said I was perfectly suited for Washington because I've always worked around nuts."

—Leon Panetta (President Clinton's White
House chief of staff), who worked in his
family walnut orchard as a child

"Washington is a city of Southern efficiency and Northern charm."

> —John Kennedy

What's Your Major?

"I'm gonna guess it was political science, but I'm not sure. It might have been history. I'll check. I hadn't thought of that one."

> —Carol Moseley Braun (2004 presidential candidate)

White House

"I would not argue I was there, and I would not argue that I was not there."

> —Christopher Dodd (senator from Connecticut, 1981–), on whether he attended political fundraisers at the White House

"I just don't have any memory of that."

> —Hillary Rodham Clinton (first lady, 1993–2001), denying under oath that she ordered the firing of the employees at the White House Travel Office

⭐ White People

"There are white niggers. I'm going to use that word."

> —Robert Byrd (senator from West Virginia, 1959–). Byrd later apologized.

"All white people, I don't believe, are intolerant. That's why I say I love the individuals, but I don't like the race."

> —Barbara-Rose Collins (representative from Michigan, 1991–1996)

"The old white boys got taken fair and square."

> —Willie Brown (mayor of San Francisco, 1996–2004), after winning an election